The STEM Crew Kids® Adventures: Building a Balloon-Powered Car

Skylar,
If you believe it,
then you can
achieve it!!
Tiffani
Teachey

TIFFANI TEACHEY

Copyright © 2023 by Tiffani Teachey
Written by Tiffani Teachey
Illustrated by Fatima Pires

All rights reserved. No part of this book may be used or reproduced in any manner whatsoever without the prior written permission of the author.

Library of Congress Control Number: 2023900780

ISBN: 978-1-7358289-9-2

Thrive Edge Publishing, LLC

I dedicate this book to my mother, Ruth Teachey, in loving memory of my father and grandfather, Bobby Teachey I and Levi E. Dixon, as well as to my brother, Bobby Teachey II. All of whom have always been by my side every step of the way. Thank you for always supporting my dreams.

In loving memory of my aunts, Mary Andrews and Edna Martin, who passed away during this book series journey. May you both rest in peace and watch over us as we make you proud.

Love,

~Tiffani Teachey

The science teacher, Mrs. Witherspoon, put the STEM Crew Kids (Ruth, Bobby, Charlie, and Emily) in the same group.

Mrs. Witherspoon assigned the group an engineering project to build a machine.

The STEM Crew Kids met in their secret treehouse to brainstorm.

Each of them had a different skill, and they made a strong team.

Bobby was good at fixing machines.

Ruth was good at designing and building new machines.

Charlie was good at conducting experiments and checking the results.

Emily was good at testing the designs to make sure they worked properly.

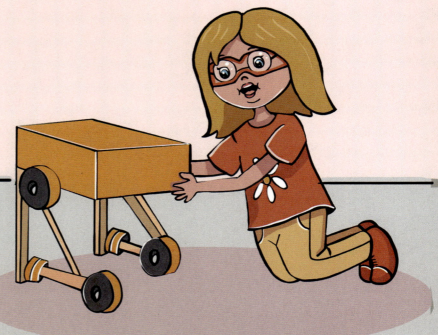

They believed they could achieve anything by working together!

After discussing briefly what they should do, Bobby said, "Ruth, you are passionate about engineering. Will you lead this project?"

Everyone else agreed.

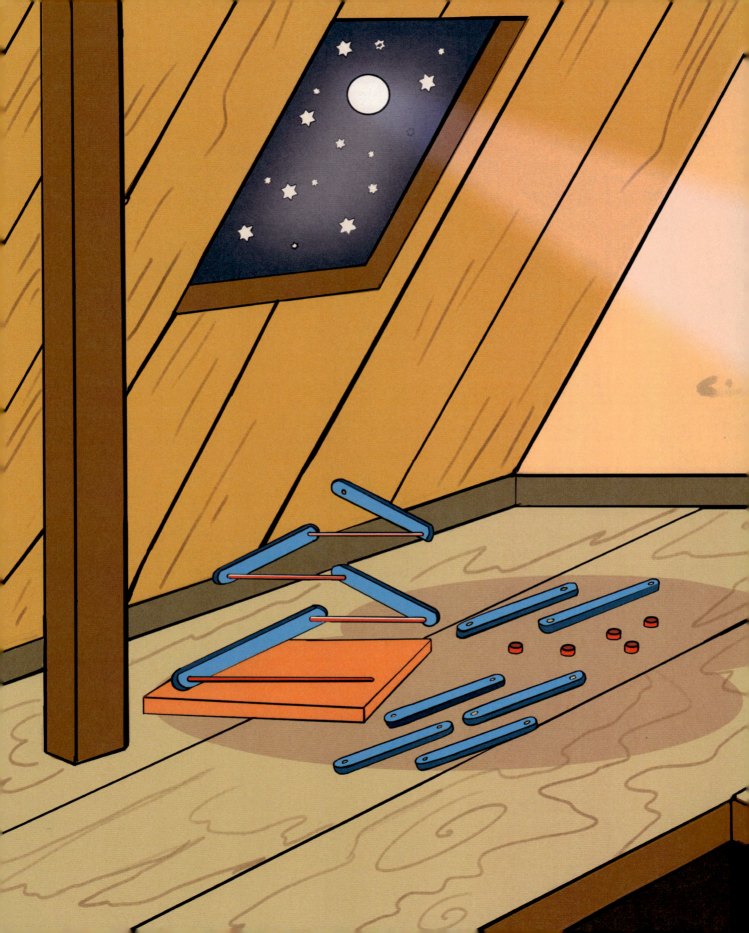

Ever since Ruth could remember, she has built and fixed gadgets.

At night, she would dash into the attic while everyone else was asleep. She had a workshop set up here to build machines.

Ruth was curious. She liked to analyze things and imagine how they worked. She wanted to be an engineer and find unique solutions to problems.

Everyone in her family knew she had a knack for fixing things. Her parents were very proud of her. When the washing machine stopped working, her mother said, "Ruth, can you fix this?" When the lawn mower stopped working, her dad said, "Ruth, can you fix this?"

Ruth loved her whole family, especially Aunty Tiffani, a mechanical engineer.

Aunty Tiffani shares in her children's book, "What Can I Be? STEM Careers from A to Z," which mechanical engineers design, build, and run machines that make power.

Aunty Tiffani visited Ruth and her family during the holidays.

When Aunty Tiffani was there, they solved problems.

They fixed the freezer when it wouldn't get cold.

They fixed the oven when it wouldn't heat food.

Aunty Tiffani always encouraged Ruth. Now Ruth wanted to be an engineer more than anything.

After science class, Ruth always looked in the trash for treasures she could take home and use to make more gadgets.

Everyone in her class thought she was the most creative engineer they knew.

When Ruth got home, she went to the attic. She thought about what machine they could build late into the night that would impress the class.

She thought of the pulley machines she had already built. She built one from LEGOs, and it raised a flag. The other one lifted snacks.

Ruth decided to go to bed. Maybe she would dream about a cool machine or think of one on her way to school.

Her mother took her to school. All the way there, Ruth tried to think of a project idea. But she still didn't have one as she walked into science class.

"Class," Mrs. Witherspoon said, "have you decided on the *gizmo* you will build?"

Silence filled the room.

Or they found what they needed in the pile of things Mrs. Witherspoon kept in the room for projects. They started building their machines.

But Ruth's group was still talking about what to build.

She only needed to come up with an original concept that none of the other kids had ever built before. She wanted to prove that one day she would be a great engineer.

Now everyone on her team was excited. They couldn't wait to begin.

When the team had everything, they asked Ruth how they would build the car.

"Well," Ruth said, "first, we must ask Mrs. Witherspoon to help us make holes in the bottle caps."

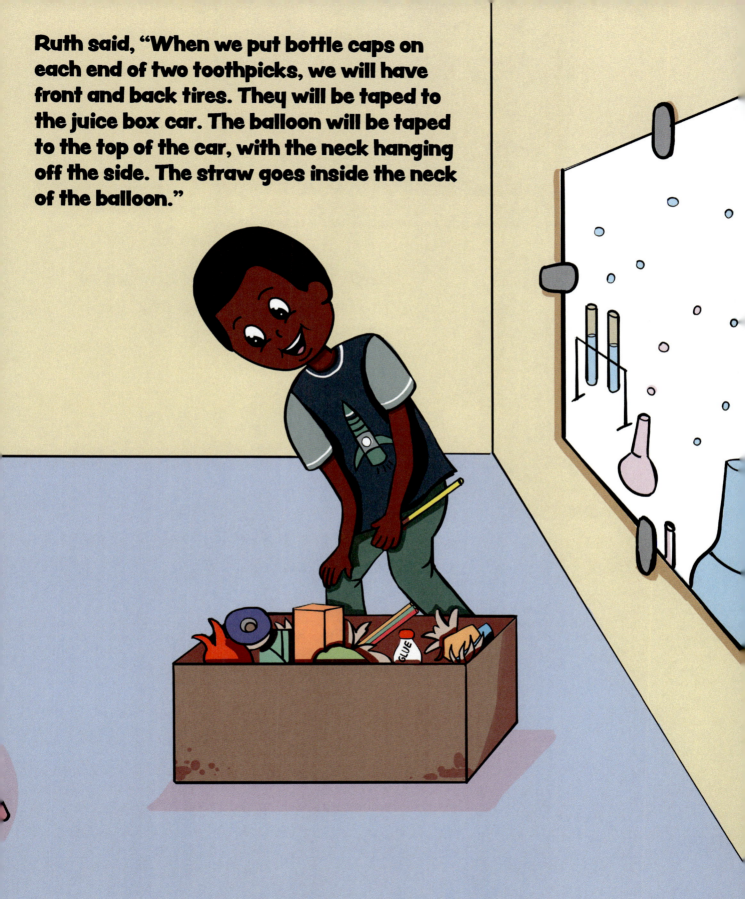

Ruth said, "When we put bottle caps on each end of two toothpicks, we will have front and back tires. They will be taped to the juice box car. The balloon will be taped to the top of the car, with the neck hanging off the side. The straw goes inside the neck of the balloon."

Ruth quickly drew a picture of the balloon-powered car. "Air will move the car forward!"

Mrs. Witherspoon put holes in the bottle caps, and the group began building their machine.

Emily tested the car after it was made so it wouldn't fall apart in the trial.

Charlie checked how fast the car was and checked the time results.

Bobby fixed the car after a bad test run.

After a few trials and errors, they were successful.

It was finally time for them to show the class their balloon-powered car.

Ruth held the car and blew air through the straw to expand the balloon. She put the car down, and it raced across the floor.

The class clapped in amazement and said, "Ooh!"

After the presentations, the other kids asked Ruth's group to teach them how to build a balloon-powered car.

Everyone smiled when Mrs. Witherspoon crowned Ruth's group the presentation winners.

Ruth was so happy! She hugged her team and told them that teamwork had made their engineering project successful.

They all celebrated by getting milkshakes after class.

That night, Ruth called Aunty Tiffani and told her about the project and said they were presentation winners.

"Well, Ruth," Aunty Tiffani said, "it looks like you are well on your way to fulfilling your dream of being an engineer!"

**The STEM Crew Kids Adventures
continues, until next time...**

ACKNOWLEDGMENTS

Thank you so much to those who supported this book.

Monica Allen
Mary Andrews
Anonymous
Reginald Archer
Naomie Baptiste
Gilda Bocock
Cynthia B. Bryant
Tamala Bullard
Julie Catalano
Cameron Clark
John Clemons
Tonya Cross
Shanta Faison
Cherie Feemster
Patricia Gause
Richard Gilliam
Lyle Gladney
Gigi Hamilton
Takia Hansley
Ross Harris
Arlena Hawthorne
Diane Hill
Sheka Houston
Ricardo Johnson
DaShaun Joseph
Marquette Kilpatrick

Dorothea Lester
Carolyn Logan
TrevisMichelle Mallard
Dawn Menge
Shadeequa Miller
Tyrie Mitchell
Constance Montgomery
Lauren Moore
Kenneth Morton
Rashan Noble
Rana O'Bryant
Zaria O'Bryant
Jennifer Parker
Ronda Pope
Melonie Robinson
Ricardo Robles
Yvette Selby
Andrea Stephenson
Carrie Teachey
Daba Thom Manuel
Aric Tucker
Stephanie Wilkins
Barbara Williams
Yancy Wingard
Charleta Wylie

Made in the USA
Middletown, DE
12 September 2023

37924068R00031